If v

# BiG BOOK of Dinosaurs

For my favourite Alice-saurus x – H.K.

A Random House book
Published by Random House Australia Pty Ltd
Level 3, 100 Pacific Highway, North Sydney NSW 2060
www.randomhouse.com.au

First published by Random House Australia in 2013

Addresses for companies within the Random House Group can be found at www.randomhouse.com.au/offices

National Library of Australia
Cataloguing-in-Publication Entry
Author: Irwin, Robert, 2003–
Title: Robert Irwin's big book of dinosaurs / Robert Irwin and Helen Kelly
ISBN: 978 1 74275 095 8 (pbk)
Subjects: Dinosaurs – Juvenile literature
Other Authors/Contributors: Kelly, Helen
Dewey Number: 567.9

Cover and internal design by Liz Seymour
Cover images: Spinosaurus © Elle Arden Images/Shutterstock; dimorphodon © Michael Rosskothen/Shutterstock; pterodactylus © Michael Rosskothen/Shutterstock

Printed in China by 1010 Printing International Ltd.

# ROBERT IRWIN
## DINOSAUR HUNTER

# BiG BOOK of Dinosaurs

RANDOM HOUSE AUSTRALIA

# CONTENTS

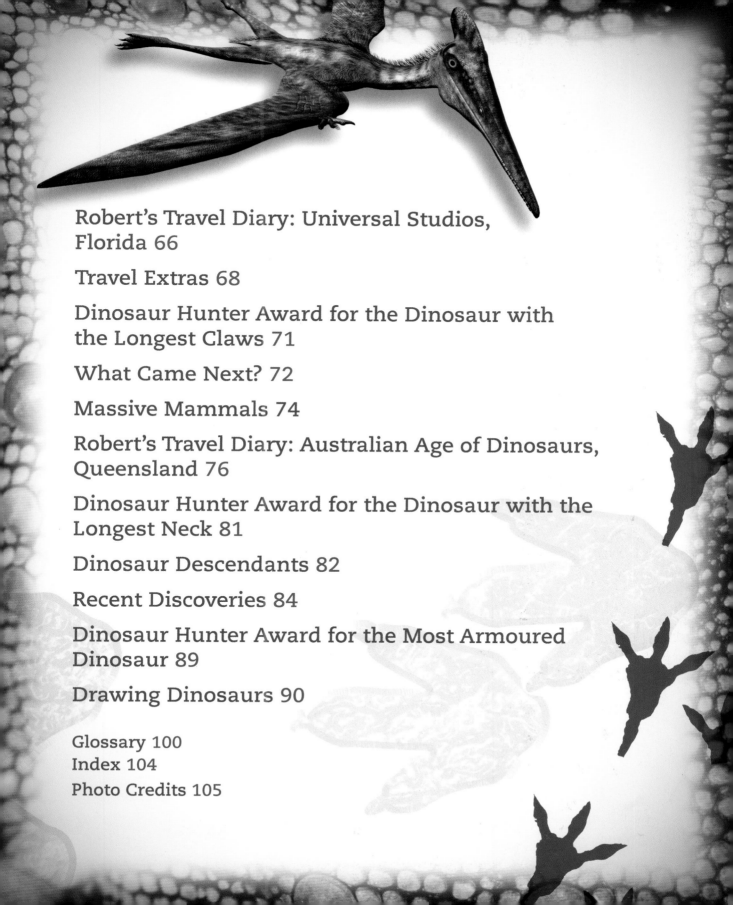

# Introducing ROBERT IRWIN, DINOSAUR HUNTER!

Robert Clarence Irwin was born on 1 December 2003. With his cheeky grin and natural curiosity, he loves nothing more than catching lizards and skinks, learning about wildlife, dinosaurs and the Australian bush, and hanging out with his much-adored sister, Bindi. Both Wildlife Warriors, Bindi and Robert received the 'Biggest Greenies' award at the Nickelodeon Kids' Choice Awards in 2009, dedicating it to their dad Steve and the Steve Irwin Wildlife Reserve (SIWR) in Cape York.

Every year, Robert is part of the annual Australia Zoo croc research trip up in far north Queensland, helping the experienced croc team to catch and tag crocodiles with tracking devices before releasing them back into the wild. Robert is super keen to learn all he can about the natural behaviours and migratory patterns of these modern-day dinosaurs.

Robert loves to draw pictures, especially of dinosaurs, and is proud that his illustrations appear in books – like this one!

He's also amassed an extensive collection of dinosaur fossils and casts, and keeps these items close to his fossicker's tool kit. As well as visiting digs around the world, Robert can count as a friend and mentor one of Australia's most eminent palaeontologists, the former Young Australian of the Year, Dr Scott Hocknull, of the Queensland Museum. Robert has also been nominated for Most Popular New Male Talent in the 2013 Logie Awards, and the Irwin family won Conservationists of the Year in the 2010 Dinosaur Ball held by the Las Vegas Natural History Museum, and were honourees in 2011 on their twentieth anniversary.

# Question Time with Robert

### What was the first dinosaur museum that you visited?

The first museum I visited was the Paris Natural History Museum in May 2005. I was only 17 months old and I loved it so much that we stayed there for the whole afternoon!

### Was there a moment when you became really interested in dinosaurs or are they something you've always been interested in?

I have always been interested in dinosaurs since I was about two or three years old. When I was first learning about dinosaurs my favourite was the T-rex, but now that I know more about the unusual dinosaurs that existed, I have new favourites.

## If you could recommend one special dinosaur museum, which one would it be and why?

All of the museums I've visited so far are pretty special, but my two favourites are:

The Lark Quarry Dinosaur Trackway, which is in Winton, Queensland. It is the largest dinosaur trackway ever recorded with more than 3000 footprints. The dinosaurs that left the tracks might have been small coelurosaurs and a large theropod dinosaur.

The American Museum of Natural History in New York. It is an awesome museum with heaps of different dinosaur species from pterosaurs to ceratopsians. Every time we visit New York I go to the museum, and at the entrance is a giant skeleton of a *Barosaurus*, which is probably one of my favourite things to see there.

# The Time of the Dinosaurs

Considering that planet Earth has been around for 4.5 billion years, it seems weird that dinosaurs were only around for 160 million of those years!

The era during which dinosaurs ruled the world is called the Mesozoic era. This era is divided up into three separate periods: the Triassic, the Jurassic and the Cretaceous.

While both the Triassic and Jurassic periods lasted for roughly 50 million years, the Cretaceous period went on for about 80 million years, but all periods ended with an event that brought about the extinction of many animal species.

Before the Triassic period, which began 251 million years ago (mya), there was plenty of life on Earth. Life had initially started out as simple bacteria and microscopic organisms that had then developed to include a huge range of reptiles, fish and insects populating the Earth, sea and air.

But it was by the end of the Triassic period that some of these reptiles had evolved into dinosaurs, or 'terrible lizards', to become the most powerful creatures the world has ever seen.

# Triassic Dinosaurs

## THE TRIASSIC PERIOD LASTED FROM 251–200 MILLION YEARS AGO

**PLANOCEPHALOSAURUS** (plan-oh-seff-el-ah-saw-rus) was a lizard-like animal that was about 20 centimetres long. It had powerful jaws and teeth for eating insects, snails and worms. Its body is almost identical to that of the tuatara, a modern-day lizard native to New Zealand.

**ICAROSAURUS** (ick-uh-row-saw-rus) was a lizard-like reptile that was only about 10 centimetres long. Its 'wings' were actually ribs covered in skin, allowing it to glide short distances.

COELOPHYSIS (cee-loh-fy-sis) was a slim and light dinosaur, possibly weighing approximately 35–40 kilograms and measuring up to about 3 metres in length. *Coelophysis* was a carnivore that preyed on small mammals and hunted in packs.

LONGISQUAMA (lon-giz-quar-ma) was another lizard-like reptile that was about 15 centimetres long. It had a straight line of stiff scales down its back that may have been feathers, though it's unclear what these scales were for.

# Jurassic Dinosaurs

## THE JURASSIC PERIOD LASTED FROM 200–145 MILLION YEARS AGO

### ALLOSAURUS

(al-oh-saw-rus) was the biggest carnivore to exist during the late Jurassic period, measuring from 5 metres in height, 12 metres in length and weighing in at around 2 tonnes. Not surprisingly, this dinosaur was at the top of the food chain, feeding off different types of dinosaurs.

### ICHTHYOSAURUS

(ick-thee-uh-saw-rus) was a marine reptile that looked a lot like a dolphin. It was fast in the water, with excellent eyesight for hunting fish. This dinosaur's nostrils were above its eyes, making it easier for *ichthyosaurus* to swim to the surface to breathe.

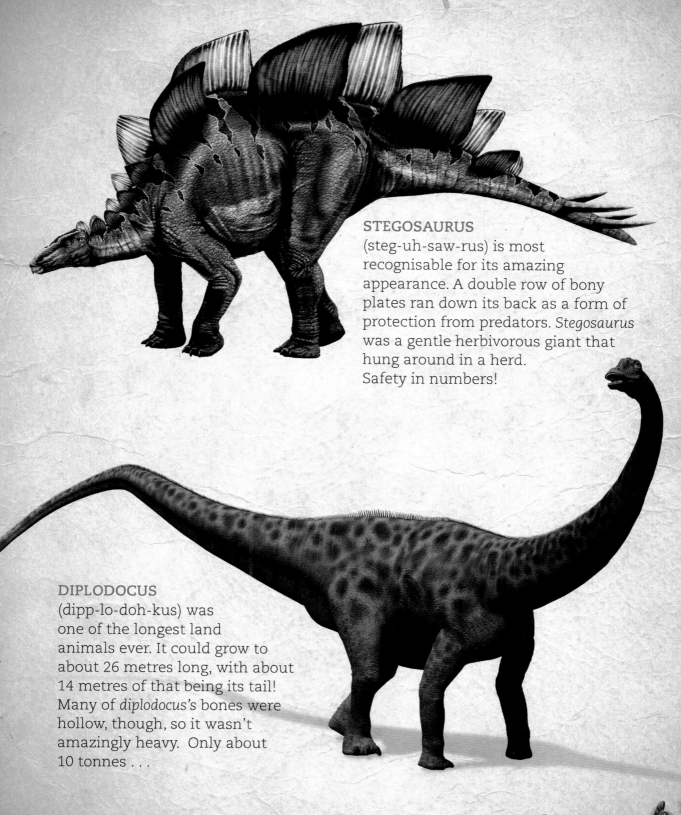

**STEGOSAURUS**
(steg-uh-saw-rus) is most recognisable for its amazing appearance. A double row of bony plates ran down its back as a form of protection from predators. *Stegosaurus* was a gentle herbivorous giant that hung around in a herd. Safety in numbers!

**DIPLODOCUS**
(dipp-lo-doh-kus) was one of the longest land animals ever. It could grow to about 26 metres long, with about 14 metres of that being its tail! Many of *diplodocus*'s bones were hollow, though, so it wasn't amazingly heavy. Only about 10 tonnes . . .

# Cretaceous Dinosaurs

## THE CRETACEOUS PERIOD LASTED FROM 145–65 MILLION YEARS AGO

**LAMBEOSAURUS** (lam-bee-oh-saw-rus) was a duck-billed dinosaur, or hadrosaur. It was a herbivore that would probably have grazed all day. *Lambeosaurus* walked on four legs, but possibly ran on two for speed. On top of its head was a solid bony spike, which might have been used as a horn for communicating with other members of the herd.

**TRICERATOPS** (tri-ser-uh-tops) is another very popular dinosaur that was gentle-natured and liked grazing in herds. *Triceratops* was pretty enormous, and would probably have made a delicious meal for a T-rex! It was built like a modern-day rhinoceros, using its great horned head to charge at its enemies. Certainly not an easy dinner choice . . .

**BARYONYX** (ba-ree-on-icks) was a scary-looking fish hunter. Its head was like that of a crocodile, and it had huge claws on its front feet. This dinosaur would have hunted along riverbanks, scooping fish out with its claws.

**TYRANNOSAURUS REX** (tie-ran-uh-saw-rus recks) is quite simply the best known and most famous dinosaur of all time. This huge predator is one of the biggest carnivores to have ever lived on land, with teeth that were around 15 centimetres long.

## The Dinosaur Hunter Award for the DINOSAUR WITH THE MOST TEETH goes to ...

# Pelecanimimus!

*Pelecanimimus* (pel-ih-can-ih-mime-us) was a small ornithomimosaur, which means 'bird-mimic lizard'. Its body shape resembled that of a modern-day ostrich.

It was only about a metre tall and 2.5 metres long, but it had a whopping 220 teeth. Most other ornithomimosaurs had no teeth at all!

Its name means 'pelican mimic' because its long snout and the pouch at its throat looked like those of the famous bird.

*Pelecanimimus* was discovered in Spain in 1993.

# Robert's

## TOP 10

# Dinosaurs

# Diamantinasaurus matildae

*D*iamantinasaurus
*matildae* was
discovered in 2005 in
central Queensland at
the Winton Formation,
one of the richest sources
of dinosaur bones in the
whole of Australia.

   *Diamantinasaurus* was a
sauropod or titanosaur – a
dinosaur that had a long neck
and tail, small head and great
big limbs. Titanosaurs were the
biggest animals to have ever lived
on land during their time.

*Diamantinasaurus* walked on four thick legs, which supported their huge weight, but were fairly small in size as far as titanosaurs go. The most well-known titanosaur would have to be *Brachiosaurus* (brack-ee-oh-saw-rus), which weighed in at 80 tonnes and was over 12 metres tall.

**Robert reckons**
Waltzing with this Matilda might crush more than just your toes!

## FACT FILE

NAME: *Diamantinasaurus matildae* (dye-ah-man-teen-ah-saw-rus mah-til-day); nicknamed 'Matilda'

MEANING: Matilda's Lizard of the Diamantina River

PERIOD: Mid Cretaceous, 100–98 million years ago (mya)

FOUND: Central Queensland

LENGTH: 15–16 metres (m)

HEIGHT: 2.5m (at the hip)

WEIGHT: 15–20 tonnes

DIET: Herbivore (plant-eater)

# Euoplocephalus

*Euoplocephalus* came from the ankylosaur family, a type of dinosaur known for their heavy armour. Thick plates of armour and spikes covered its upper body and limbs, leaving just its soft underbelly unprotected. Its head was like a large box made from bone with thick spikes shielding the sides of its face – even its eyes were protected by bone eyelids! At the end of *euoplocephalus's* muscular tail was a huge ball of bone, which was a useful weapon that could kill attackers with one good swing. Considering the size of the *euoplocephalus's* body, its brain was small and it wouldn't have been as intelligent as other dinosaurs. *Euoplocephalus* may have spent its days grazing, needing enormous amounts of food to keep its huge body going.

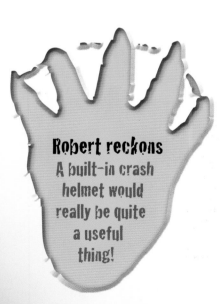

**Robert reckons**
A built-in crash helmet would really be quite a useful thing!

## FACT FILE

NAME: *Euoplocephalus*
(you-oh-ploe-keff-ah-luss)

MEANING: Well-armoured head

PERIOD: Late Cretaceous, 73mya

FOUND: Montana, USA and Canada

LENGTH: 6m

HEIGHT: 2m

WEIGHT: 2 tonnes

DIET: Herbivore

# Albertaceratops

*A*lbertaceratops belonged to a group of herbivorous dinosaurs called the ceratopsians. They were remarkable for the way their huge heads were armoured and horned for protection. *Albertaceratops* had a bony ridge over its nose and a huge frill, made of bone, around its neck and shoulders, with two large

hooked horns that pointed outwards. They also had parrot-like beaks and powerful jaws that could eat even the toughest plants. *Albertaceratops* thrived for a long time and lived together in herds.

**Robert reckons**
With *albertosaurus* and *albertaceratops* both coming from there, Alberta is definitely on my 'favourite places to visit' list!

# Anhanguera

*Anhanguera* was a large pterosaur (flying reptile) of the Cretaceous period, so although it wasn't a dinosaur, *anhanguera* was a big presence all the same. It had a long, crested beak and a long neck but very small legs. This flying reptile was splayfooted, so it would've been a very clumsy walker on land! But *anhanguera* was built to fly, and its skin-covered wings had a 4-metre wingspan. Its bones were thin and light, making the flying reptile aerodynamic. *Anhanguera's* diet mainly consisted of fish, and it flew with its head angled down towards the water so it could catch them easily. Lots of needle-thin teeth made sure that when *anhanguera* caught fish by skimming the surface of the water, there was no chance of the prey falling out.

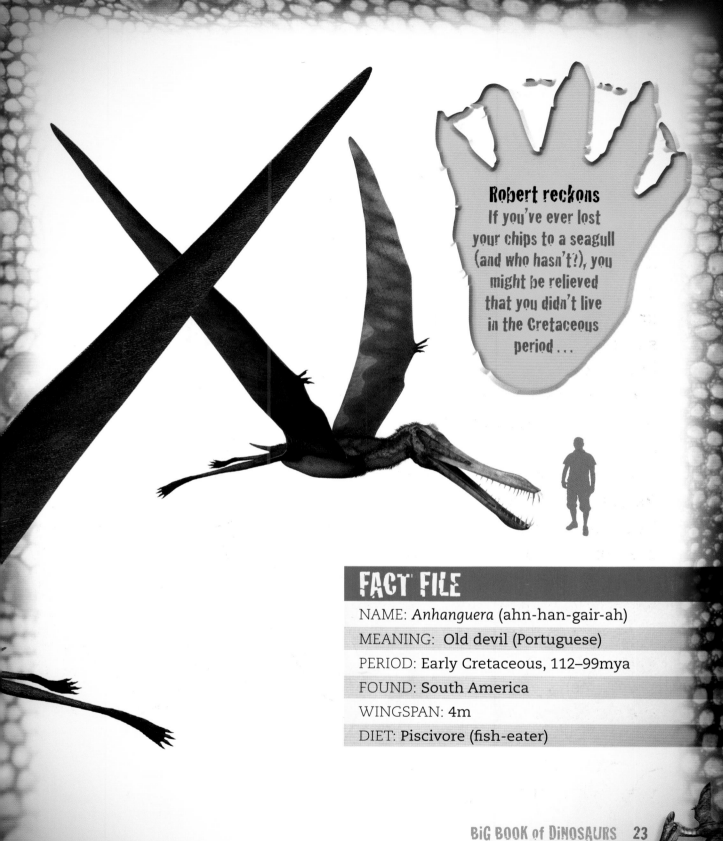

**Robert reckons**
If you've ever lost your chips to a seagull (and who hasn't?), you might be relieved that you didn't live in the Cretaceous period . . .

## FACT FILE

NAME: *Anhanguera* (ahn-han-gair-ah)

MEANING: Old devil (Portuguese)

PERIOD: Early Cretaceous, 112–99mya

FOUND: South America

WINGSPAN: 4m

DIET: Piscivore (fish-eater)

# Parasaurolophus

Parasaurolophus belonged to a group of duck-billed dinosaurs that were called hadrosaurs. They had a broad mouth that was toothless at the front, but the most eye-catching thing about *parasaurolophus* was the long, hollow, horn-like crest that ran from their snouts up beyond the top of their heads. This crest was almost 2 metres long and it's still unclear what its purpose was; palaeontologists have decided that it definitely was not used as a snorkel or as a weapon. It's likely that this crest was used to make a trumpeting call that could attract a mate.

*Parasaurolophus* was happy to wander around on four legs but could run on two if speed was needed.

## FACT FILE

NAME: *Parasaurolophus* (para-saw-roll-oh-fus)

MEANING: Near crested lizard

PERIOD: Late Cretaceous, 76–73mya

FOUND: North America

LENGTH: 9.5m

WEIGHT: 2.5 tonnes

DIET: Herbivore

# Argentinosaurus

rgentinosaurus was discovered in 1988 and very little information has actually been found at all. But based on the few bones that were unearthed – a 1.5-metre long tibia (leg bone) and a 1.6-metre long vertebra – palaeontologists believe that this was the biggest and heaviest land animal to ever walk the planet. Eating their way through 3 tonnes of

vegetation a day, they would've had to keep on the move almost constantly to find food.

When *argentinosaurus* young hatched from their eggs, they weighed just 5 kilograms and were left completely to their own devices. Luckily they were already equipped with teeth, so they could start eating straight-away. And they grew quickly, going from 5 kilograms to 7500 kilograms in just 25 years!

## FACT FILE

NAME: *Argentinosaurus*
(ar-jen-teen-ah-saw-rus)

MEANING: Lizard of Argentina

PERIOD: Late Cretaceous, 97–94mya

FOUND: South America

LENGTH: 36m

HEIGHT: Approx. 21m

WEIGHT: 60–88 tonnes

DIET: Herbivore

**Robert reckons**
Can't wait until they find all the bones in this dinosaur puzzle. It is definitely one I need to see!

# Spinosaurus

Spinosaurus was a distinctive-looking creature with a huge crest running down the length of its back. This crest or sail was made from bones, and it's unclear whether it was used for controlling the dinosaur's temperature or whether it was just for display, like a peacock's tail. The bones themselves were about 1.5 metres long.

Spinosaurus could definitely win the title of both the biggest and heaviest carnivorous dinosaur ever!

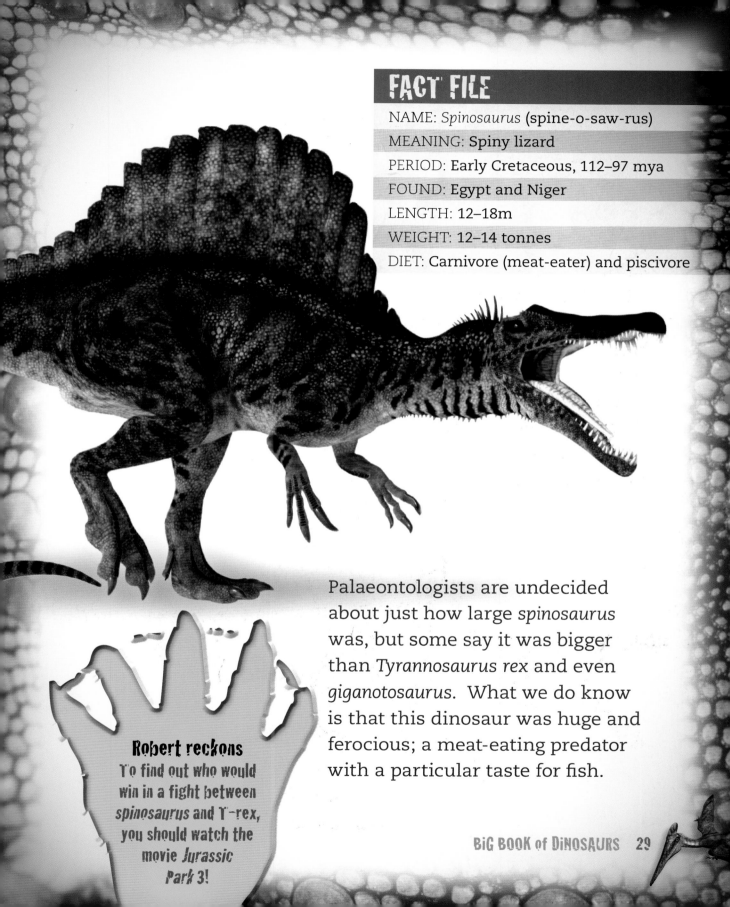

## FACT FILE

**NAME:** *Spinosaurus* (spine-o-saw-rus)

**MEANING:** Spiny lizard

**PERIOD:** Early Cretaceous, 112–97 mya

**FOUND:** Egypt and Niger

**LENGTH:** 12–18m

**WEIGHT:** 12–14 tonnes

**DIET:** Carnivore (meat-eater) and piscivore

Palaeontologists are undecided about just how large *spinosaurus* was, but some say it was bigger than *Tyrannosaurus rex* and even *giganotosaurus*. What we do know is that this dinosaur was huge and ferocious; a meat-eating predator with a particular taste for fish.

**Robert reckons**
To find out who would win in a fight between *spinosaurus* and T-rex, you should watch the movie *Jurassic Park 3!*

# Sarcosuchus

*S*arcosuchus was a distant ancestor of the crocodile and a member of a huge family of crocodylia (large reptiles) that dates back 230 million years. This dinosaur was enormous, weighing in at roughly 8 tonnes and measuring 12 metres in length. That's

**Robert reckons**
A life-size model of sarcosuchus would make an awesome birthday present for a 9-year-old boy!

about twice the size of the biggest saltwater croc you'd see today! The skull itself was about the length of an average human, with most of that made up of its snout and jaws. *Sarcosuchus* had 132 thick teeth, which were put to good use munching on fish, turtles and the occasional dinosaur that wandered too close to the shoreline.

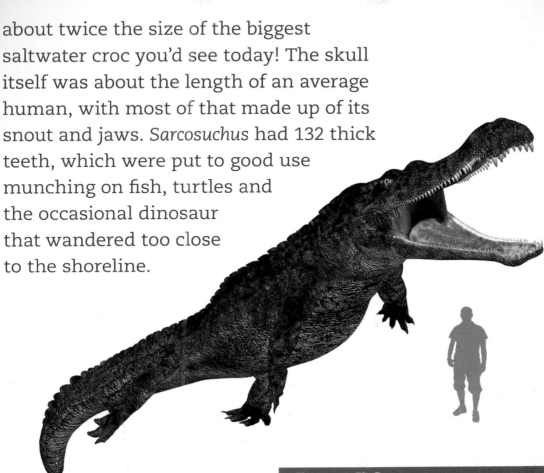

## FACT FILE

NAME: *Sarcosuchus* (sar-ko-soo-kus)

MEANING: Flesh crocodile

PERIOD: Early Cretaceous, 112mya

FOUND: Africa and South America

LENGTH: 12m

WEIGHT: 8 tonnes

DIET: Carnivore and piscivore

# Muttaburrasaurus

**M**uttaburrasaurus was first discovered in Australia in 1981, in a town called Muttaburra, after which it was named. It was a large herbivorous dinosaur that looked a lot like an *Iguanodon* but with a different shaped head. Although the *muttaburrasaurus* stood upright on its hind legs and had shorter forelimbs, it could walk on either two or four legs. It also had a large hollow bump on its nose in front of its eyes, though it's unclear what purpose this bony bump had. *Muttaburrasaurus* had very strong jaws and super-sharp teeth that could munch through the toughest vegetation, such as ferns and cycads.

**Robert reckons**

If you should ever find yourself in Hughenden, a little outback town in Queensland, look up. You'll see a huge statue of this guy!

## FACT FILE

**NAME:** *Muttaburrasaurus* (mutt-ah-burr-ah-saw-rus)

**MEANING:** Lizard of Muttaburra

**PERIOD:** Early Cretaceous, 112–98mya

**FOUND:** Queensland

**LENGTH:** 8m

**WEIGHT:** 2.5 tonnes

**DIET:** Herbivore

# Australovenator

<big>A</big>ustralovenator wintonensis is a newcomer to the Australian dinosaur scene. It was only discovered in 2009 and belonged to the allosaur family – carnivorous dinosaurs that could walk on two feet. Australovenator was small for an allosaur, measuring just under 2 metres at the hip and 6 metres in length, and weighed somewhere between 500 and 1000 kilograms. But don't let its size fool you – this dinosaur was a deadly predator. Australovenator has been called the 'cheetah' of its time for its speed and agility, even though it ran on two legs and not four. This dinosaur had three long slashing claws on each hand as well as razor-sharp teeth.

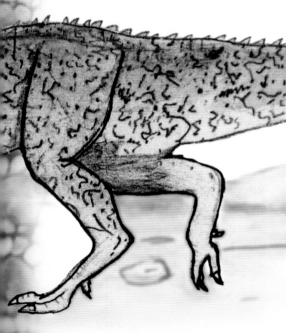

## FACT FILE

NAME: *Australovenator wintonensis*
(oss-tra-low-ven-ah-tor win-ton-en-sis)

MEANING: Southern hunter

PERIOD: Early Cretaceous, 112–99mya

FOUND: Winton, Queensland

LENGTH: 6m

WEIGHT: 500–1000kg

DIET: Carnivore

*Drawn by Robert Irwin*

**Robert reckons**
*Australovenator* is just so cool and, coming from Queensland, we're practically neighbours! He really deserves the no. 1 spot!

# MUSEUM OF NATURAL HISTORY, LONDON

The Museum of Natural History in London is just fantastic. It's really old and looks like it would be super spooky after dark. It's been open since 1881 and has over 70 million items to look at. It's so old that some of the items there were collected by Charles Darwin himself!

It would have taken weeks to see all the items, so we concentrated on my favourite bits – the dinosaurs!

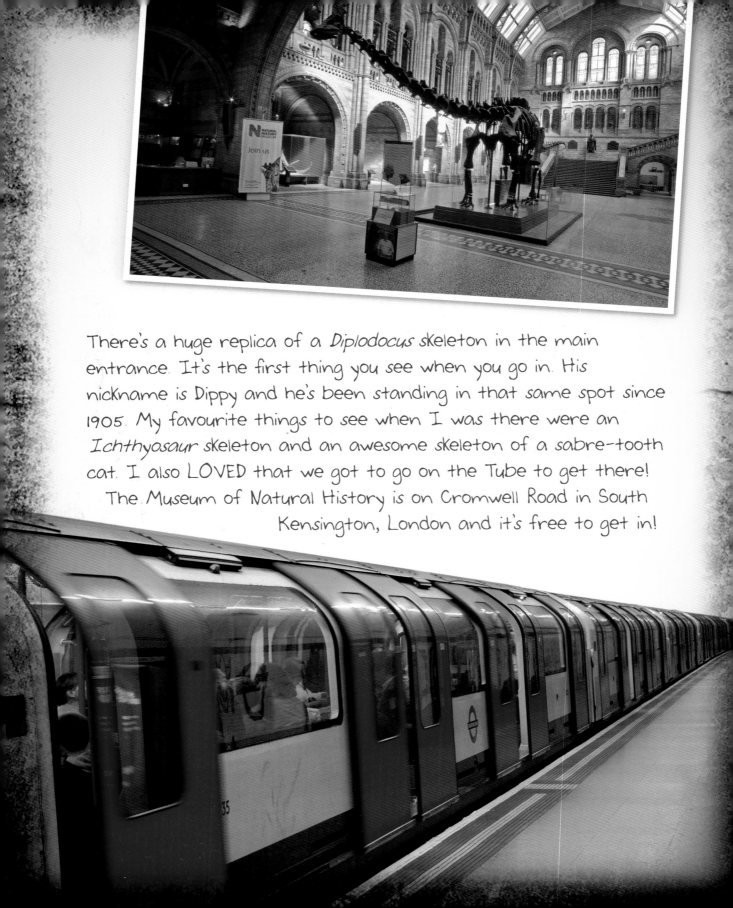

There's a huge replica of a *Diplodocus* skeleton in the main entrance. It's the first thing you see when you go in. His nickname is Dippy and he's been standing in that same spot since 1905. My favourite things to see when I was there were an *Ichthyosaur* skeleton and an awesome skeleton of a sabre-tooth cat. I also LOVED that we got to go on the Tube to get there! The Museum of Natural History is on Cromwell Road in South Kensington, London and it's free to get in!

# AUSTRALIA THROUGH TIME

## Changing world

Our planet hasn't always looked the way it does today. The Earth is constantly changing, and if we go back as far as the time of the earliest dinosaurs, we can see just how much our planet has been transformed over the years.

The continents themselves move and shift with time. This phenomenon is called continental drift, and it was first suggested as a geological possibility by a German scientist called Alfred Wegener in the early twentieth century. He noticed that the edges of all the continents, as they are now, looked like those of a huge jigsaw puzzle. He thought that if you were to move these large pieces of land together they would fit pretty well, and that at some point in the distant past they had all formed one huge landmass.

But because no-one took Wegener's theory seriously, the continental drift wasn't officially recognised as a scientific explanation for the continents' movement through time until the 1960s.

Earth as a complete whole, comprising all the continents we know today, is called Pangaea, which is Greek for 'all Earth'. This supercontinent was surrounded by a huge ocean called Panthalassa, meaning 'all seas'.

Gradually, over the next 100 million years, Pangaea split in two, and by the end of the Jurassic period, there were two new smaller supercontinents: Laurasia and Gondwana.

Laurasia was the northern continent and contained North America, Europe and Asia. Gondwana was the southern continent and was made up of South America, Africa, India, Antarctica and Australia. The two were separated by the Tethys Sea.

It wasn't until the late Cretaceous period that the map of the world started to look a bit more familiar. The two big landmasses had broken up into smaller ones and all the continents had drifted into a formation that is far more recognisable today.

Though continental drift might sound like a calm series of smooth moves, it's not necessarily that simple. As the continents move and separate they also collide with each other. For instance, when India collided with Asia some 70 million years ago to become part of that continent, the impact was so huge that it created the Himalayas.

The whole process causes upheaval all over the Earth, creating a lot of volcanic eruptions, earthquakes and climate change. The continents continue to drift today, with Australia inching northwards at a rate of 10 millimetres per year. Some scientists think that in another 250 million years, the world might resemble Pangaea again.

# Changing Australia

It was during the Cretaceous period that Gondwana's landmass slowly began to fracture and separate. India broke away and drifted off about 130 million years ago, followed by New Zealand 50 million years later.

When you think about how hot it now is in Australia and how cold it is in Antarctica, it seems a bit weird that Antarctica was the last big land-mass to go its own way. But Australia only separated from Antarctica about 53 million years ago. And while Australia went north to become one of the hottest, driest continents on the planet, Antarctica drifted south and the first ice started to form on it shortly after. By 15 million years ago, this icy continent was pretty much as it is now: 98% of Antarctica's land-

mass is covered in ice that's about 1.5 kilometres thick!

As the land broke into smaller and smaller pieces, the differences between dinosaurs in various areas became greater. These creatures had to adapt to changing environments and climates or face the consequences.

As a result, many dinosaurs that lived in Australia developed quite differently to some of their earlier relations in the rest of the world.

**Minmi** or **Minmi paravertebra** (minmee par-ah-verr-tuh-bra) had longer legs, possibly making it a better runner than its fellow ankylosaurs.

*Leaellynasaura* (lee-el-in-uh-saw-ruh) had huge eyes, which possibly meant it could see better during the long dark winters. While Australia was still attached to Antarctica, it would have been dark for up to three months of the year!

**Australovenator** was about half the size of its more famous cousin *allosaurus*, but the reason for this is still unknown.

# DINOSAUR HUNTER AWARDS

## The Dinosaur Hunter Award for the SMALLEST DINOSAUR goes to ...

# Microraptor!

*Microraptor* (my-crow-rap-torr) was an extremely small dinosaur that was less than a metre long, and weighed only 1 kilogram. Its name in Greek means 'small thief'.

Its body was covered in feathers and its most amazing feature was its two sets of primitive wings – located on its forearms and hindlegs – which *microraptor* used to glide about from tree to tree. It also had a long tail, which was tipped with a diamond-shaped feathered fan.

*Microraptor* lived during the early Cretaceous period, around 145–130 million years ago.

Some scientists argue that *microraptor* was capable of flight, which makes for one tiny but flighty dinosaur!

# AMERICAN MUSEUM OF NATURAL HISTORY, NEW YORK

The American Museum of Natural History is another one of those really old, spooky museums. It opened in 1877 and sits in Central Park. It's got so many different species of dinosaur! You'll find everything from pterosaurs to ceratopsians. My absolute favourite bit is when you first walk into the building and there's a huge *Barosaurus* skeleton up on its hind legs. When I was little, I thought it must've been the biggest creature in the whole world! I always visit this museum whenever I go to New York – it's just so cool.

You'll find the American Museum of Natural History on Central Park West at 79th Street, New York City, United States of America.

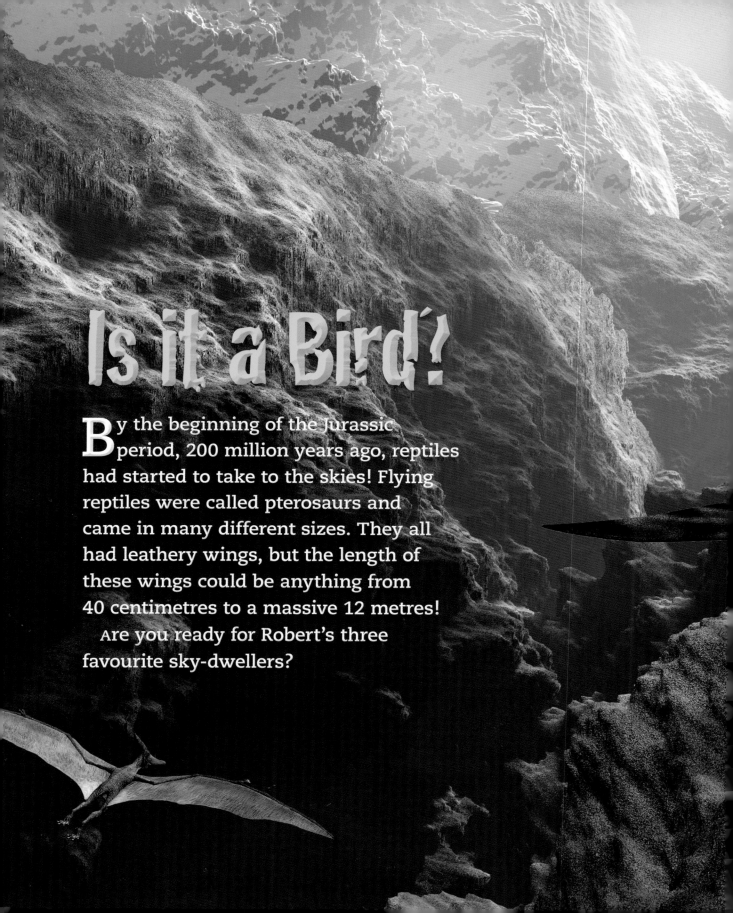

# Is it a Bird?

**B**y the beginning of the Jurassic period, 200 million years ago, reptiles had started to take to the skies! Flying reptiles were called pterosaurs and came in many different sizes. They all had leathery wings, but the length of these wings could be anything from 40 centimetres to a massive 12 metres!

Are you ready for Robert's three favourite sky-dwellers?

# Dimorphodon

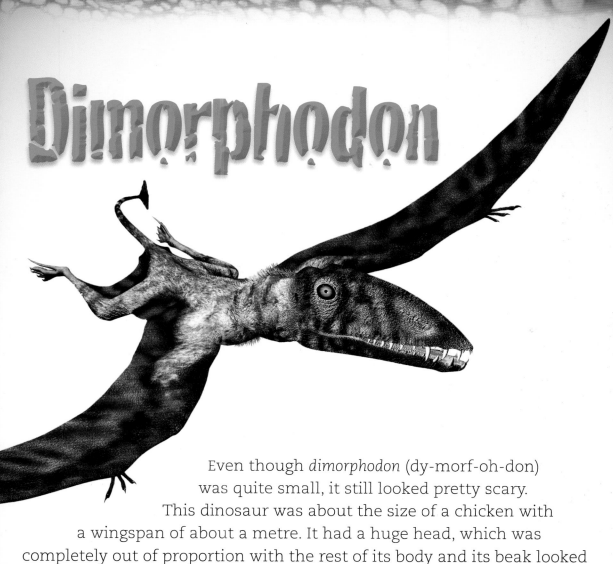

Even though *dimorphodon* (dy-morf-oh-don) was quite small, it still looked pretty scary. This dinosaur was about the size of a chicken with a wingspan of about a metre. It had a huge head, which was completely out of proportion with the rest of its body and its beak looked just like a puffin's.

*Dimorphodon* lived in Europe during the early Jurassic period, and although it's not clear what their diet consisted of, they most likely fed on insects or small lizards. *Dimorphodon* was named after the two different types of teeth it had, the Greek translation of which is 'two shape teeth'.

# Pteranodon

*Pteranodon* (terr-an-oh-don) had a huge wingspan. The biggest males were estimated to have had wingspans as broad as 7 metres. It comes as no surprise then that these dinosaurs were amazing flyers with excellent eyesight for spotting a good meal miles below. The long hollow crests on the back of their heads were possibly used like rudders, for steering and keeping them stable when they changed direction.

Like *dimorphodon*, *pteranodon* got its name from a couple of Greek words, in this case, 'ptera' meaning 'winged' and 'nodon' meaning 'toothless'. Who would have guessed that this scary-looking reptile had no teeth! *Pteranodons* caught and ate fish much like a pelican would today.

# Archaeopteryx

Although *archaeopteryx* (ark-e-op-ter-rix) technically isn't a dinosaur, it was the first bird to fly around the Jurassic skies. It looked very much like a modern bird, with feathers and a long bony but feathered tail. Some pictures tend to show *archaeopteryx* with colourful feathers, though in actual fact it's not really clear what colour it was. It had small sharp teeth and is thought to have fed on insects. This prehistoric bird wasn't very big at all – just about the size of a modern-day magpie.

# DINOSAUR HUNTER AWARDS

The Dinosaur
Hunter Award
for the MOST WEIRD-LOOKING
DINOSAUR goes to . . .

# Pegomastax!

*Pegomastax* (peg-oh-mass-tacks) was a little dinosaur, not much bigger than a household cat.

It looks so fearsome, with its body covered in quills, that *pegomastax* has been nicknamed 'the Dracula dinosaur'!

It had a parrot-like beak with two long vampirish fangs at the bottom. And just to make it even more dangerous, the fangs were serrated! An odd sort of accessory for a herbivore . . .

# ROBERT'S TRAVEL DIARY

# KRONOSAURUS KORNER, QUEENSLAND

This is one of my favourite museums ever! It's in Queensland, so you might think that it's close to us at Australia Zoo, but it's actually about 1650 kilometres away! So I don't get to go there as often as

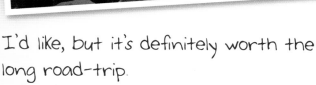

I'd like, but it's definitely worth the long road-trip.

Richmond is a little outback town with about 750 people living in it. The museum has been there since 1989 and was built when a farmer discovered fossils on his land. These fossils turned out to be an almost complete skeleton of a *Pliosaur*. It was 102 million years old! Back then, all of the middle of Australia would have been taken up with the Eromanga Sea, so the whole area would have been under water.

This museum is packed with fossils of lots of marine reptiles as well as those of the Australian dinosaur *Minmi*.

There's a cool area nearby where you can dig about for your own fossils. They call it 'fossicking'. If you find something, the people from the preparation lab will tell you exactly what it is and how old it is. You could find a real fossil from the dinosaur era! We had a good dig, with fossils from *ichthyosaurs*, *elasmosauruses* and more.

You can find Kronosaurus Korner at 91-93 Goldring Street, Richmond, Queensland.

# There's Something in the Water!

**L**ong, long before dinosaurs walked the Earth, life started out in the oceans. Bit by bit, as billions of years passed, the tiny microscopic organisms that lived in our oceans grew into much bigger and more complex organisms. By 500 million years ago, some of those organisms had evolved into large sea creatures with backbones. Robert's favourite prehistoric sea-dwellers came a bit later.

# Liopleurodon

*Liopleurodon* (ly-oh-ploo-ro-don) was a huge carnivorous marine reptile from the mid Jurassic period. It looked a lot like a whale with a thick streamlined body, short neck and four huge paddle-like flippers, which enabled it to swim fast and turn quickly. *Liopleurodon* put its speed to good use in chasing its prey, which were normally large sea creatures such as sharks and *Ichthyosaurs* (another marine reptile that looked very much like a dolphin). *Liopleurodon* attacked them with its powerful jaws and strong teeth.

# Elasmosaurus

*Elasmosaurus* (e-laz-muh-saw-rus) belonged to a family of marine reptiles called plesiosaurs and was the longest member in the family, measuring at approximately 14 metres. About half that length was its neck! It had a tiny head but mighty jaws and sharp teeth for catching and eating fish as well as other small marine animals. Although their feet looked a lot like a turtle's flippers, it's now thought that plesiosaurs moved through the water more like penguins than turtles. They lived in the open oceans of the late Cretaceous period.

# Archelon

*Archelon* (ark-eh-lon) is Greek for 'ruler turtle', so there's no doubt at all this was the biggest sea turtle that ever lived! It was about 4 metres long and 2 tonnes in weight, so roughly the same size as your family car. *Archelon*'s flat shell was different to other turtles' because it wasn't made of bone but of a leathery type of skin. Its closest relative today is the leatherback turtle and it's thought that they even shared the same diet. *Archelon*'s beaks were toothless, so they were quite limited in what they could eat – luckily, jellyfish and squid didn't need much chewing.

# DINOSAUR HUNTER AWARDS

## The Dinosaur Hunter Award for the DINOSAUR MADE MOST FAMOUS BY HOLLYWOOD goes to ...

# Velociraptor!

With a name meaning 'swift thief', it was no surprise that Hollywood chose this dinosaur for a starring role in the movie *Jurassic Park*.

In the film, *velociraptor* (veh-loss-ih-rap-tor) was portrayed as a huge predator, intelligent and cunning. A huge sickle-shaped claw on its hind leg was the ultimate slashing weapon.

But the reality was a little different. While the scary claw did exist, *velociraptor* was only less than a metre tall and weighed in at just 15 kilograms!

It lived during the late Cretaceous period in what is now Mongolia.

# UNIVERSAL STUDIOS, FLORIDA

Now, when your sister is a film star you get the chance to go to a lot of exciting places. We were in Florida, celebrating the release of *Free Willy: Escape from Pirate's Cove*, which starred the one and only Bindi Irwin, but we took some time out to squeeze in a dinosaur or two at Universal Studios. They were so realistic!

# ROBERT'S TRAVEL DIARY

Of course, there are other places that are rich with dinosaur fossils and history. Here's a couple of great locations ...

# NATIONAL MUSEUM OF NATURAL HISTORY, FRANCE

# AUSTRALIAN MUSEUM, SYDNEY

# DINOSAUR HUNTER AWARDS

## The Dinosaur Hunter Award for the DINOSAUR WITH THE LONGEST CLAWS goes to ...

# Therizinosaurus!

The name means 'scythe lizard', and *therizinosaurus* (thair-uh-zeen-uh-sawr-us) was well-equipped with these deadly cutting tools in the form of its claws.

Though it was certainly big, possibly up to 10 metres long, the three huge claws it had on each forelimb were way out of proportion with the rest of its body. Each claw was about 80 centimetres long, almost straight and tapered to a deadly point at the tip.

We don't know what *therizinosaurus* might have eaten, but it could have been herbivorous, using its immense claws to gather leaves and branches.

*Therizinosaurus* lived during the late Cretaceous period, around 70 million years ago.

# What Came Next?

Dinosaurs disappeared from Earth many million years ago. Scientists are still not completely sure why they became extinct so suddenly, but some think it was due to a huge number of volcanoes erupting at the same time and poisoning the air. Others think that the meteor that hit our planet 65 million years ago might be the cause.

The meteor was more than 10 kilometres wide and would have hit the Earth at an incredible speed, exploding with the force of a zillion atom bombs. The dust and debris it threw up would have blocked out the sun from Earth for years and years. Without the nourishment of the sun, many of the plants would have died. The dinosaurs that fed on the plants would have perished from lack of food, and in turn the dinosaurs that fed on the plant-eating dinosaurs would eventually have starved too.

But not everything was completely wiped out. Some insects and animals survived, such as frogs, snakes and crocodiles. But most importantly for us, mammals survived too.

It was the beginning of the Age of Mammals and the emergence of megafauna.

# Massive Mammals

Megafauna are large warm-blooded animals that evolved and adapted to the Earth's conditions, shortly after dinosaurs became extinct. These massive mammals were a lot more common during the Cenozoic era, around 65 to 2 million years ago, with a few continuing to exist beyond that era. Here are some megafauna that are ancestors of popular animals we know today.

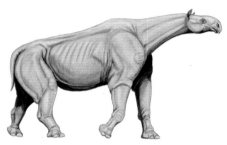

**Indricotherium** (*in-drik-oh-thee-ree-um*)
Ancestor of the rhinoceros
PERIOD: 33–23 mya
LENGTH: Approx. 9m
HEIGHT: 7m
WEIGHT: 15–30 tonnes
SPECIAL FEATURES: It had a long neck, which could stretch up to the highest branches, and a long, flexible upper lip to grab leaves and tear them off the trees. Indricotherium was the largest land mammal to have ever existed.

**Glyptodon** (*glip-toh-don*)
Ancestor of the armadillo
PERIOD: 2mya to about 15,000 years ago
LENGTH: 3m
HEIGHT: 1.5m
WEIGHT: 1 tonne
SPECIAL FEATURES:
A rounded shell – made up of over a thousand separate bony plates – protected this mammal from predators and a bony cap on top of its skull made for great armoured headgear.

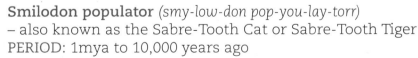

**Smilodon populator** (*smy-low-don pop-you-lay-torr*)
– also known as the Sabre-Tooth Cat or Sabre-Tooth Tiger
PERIOD: 1mya to 10,000 years ago
LENGTH: 2.6m
WEIGHT: Approx. 400kg
SPECIAL FEATURES: *Smilodon's* stand-out feature was two huge canine teeth that sat on either side of its mouth. They were sharp and serrated, which explains the name Smilodon; meaning 'knife tooth' in Greek.

## Megatherium (mega-thee-ree-um)
### – meaning 'great beast'
### Ancestor of the echidna or anteater
PERIOD: 3mya to 10,500 years ago
LENGTH: 6m
WEIGHT: Up to 4 tonnes
SPECIAL FEATURES: It had large backwards-facing claws on its feet to help with ripping off, although this made walking difficult, so this great beast walked on the outside edges of its feet. *Megatherium* also had a large muscular tail, which acted like a tripod to support its body when reaching up high.

## Woolly mammoth
### (woo-lee mah-muth)
### Ancestor of the elephant
PERIOD: 5mya to 4,500 years ago
HEIGHT: 2.5–4m
WEIGHT: 6–10 tonnes
SPECIAL FEATURES:
The *woolly mammoth* was covered in thick brown orangey fur to combat the freezing temperatures of the Ice Age. Their tusks were also much larger than those of modern-day elephants and could be straight or curved.

# ROBERT'S TRAVEL DIARY

# AUSTRALIAN AGE OF DINOSAURS, QUEENSLAND

The Australian Age of Dinosaurs museum is in a little town called Winton, Queensland. It's more than just a museum – it's the biggest fossil preparation laboratory in the southern hemisphere. It has the largest

collection of Australian dinosaur bones anywhere in the world! And they were all found in what's known as the Winton Formation. It's right in the middle of the outback and it looks like there's nothing but red sandy desert for miles around. The people are super-friendly and show you all the fossils that they are preparing. They even let me and Bindi have a go at digging and at scratching away at a fossil with an air-scribe! We saw Banjo the *Australovenator,* Matilda the *Diamantinasaurus,* and Clancy, a *Wintonotitan;* all three are the first of their species to be discovered.

*This is us with David and Judy Elliott. They run the museum and find the fossils!*

About 100 kilometres away is Lark Quarry Conservation Park, a place where it's believed a huge dinosaur stampede took place. There are about 3,300 perfectly preserved footprints in the small area and it's pretty cool to see. They're all shapes and sizes and some could well have belonged to my favourite dinosaur *australovenator* as he chased down some coelurosaurs for dinner!

If you should ever find yourself in Winton, just ask for directions to The Jump-Up. You'll have an awesome time!

# DINOSAUR HUNTER AWARDS

## The Dinosaur Hunter Award for DINOSAUR WITH THE LONGEST NECK goes to . . .

# Tanystropheus!

The name means 'long vertebra', and this lengthy backbone certainly helped this reptile stick its neck out!

Its neck, made up of ten bones, measured up to about 3 metres and was longer than its tail and body put together. *Tanystropheus* (tan-is-troh-fee-us) seems to have been a land-dwelling animal that lived on the shores of rivers and seas, stretching its neck out as a fishing rod to catch food at the water's edge.

It lived during the middle Triassic period, about 232 million years ago.

# Dinosaur Descendants

We all know that dinosaurs are extinct, but some of Robert's favourite modern-day creatures resemble them a lot. Many of them are remote descendants of animals that existed long before the dinosaurs and were lucky enough to survive whatever killed off those huge ruling reptiles. This includes:

- Crocodiles
- Komodo dragons
- Alligators
- Snakes
- Insects (especially cockroaches!)
- Tuatara (a lizard-like reptile from New Zealand)
- Horseshoe crabs
- Sharks

Sometimes, it pays to be small . . .

# Recent Discoveries

## CHINA, 2008

### DINOSAURS STOP WORK IN ZHUCHENG

Workers digging on the outskirts of the city of Zhucheng unearthed what they claim to be the biggest deposit of dinosaur bones ever found. Around 7,600 fossils have been discovered so far, dating back 100 million years to the Cretaceous period. The haul includes a pterosaur, as well as the skull of a ceratopsian and the skeleton of an ankylosaurus.

# MONGOLIA, 2010

## LONG-LOST COUSIN DISCOVERED

On a field trip to Inner Mongolia, a British student uncovered an almost complete skeleton of a meat-eating bird-like dinosaur from the late Cretaceous period. *Linheraptor* (linn-her-rapt-orr) was fast and agile on its feet, weighing only 25 kilograms and was approximately 2 metres in length. A long curved toe-claw on each foot resembles that of its famous cousin, the *velociraptor*.

**BRAZIL, 2011**
A new type of ancient crocodile has been discovered with the unearthing of an almost complete skull. *Pepesuchus deiseae* lived 99–65 million years ago.

# CANADA, 2012

## ALIEN DISCOVERED IN ALBERTA

Canadian palaeontologists have discovered a new species of horned dinosaur in southern Alberta. The ceratopsian, the most primitive of its kind discovered so far, has been called *Xenoceratops* (zen-o-serra-tops), which is Greek for 'alien horned face'. And it seems quite a fitting name for a creature with a parrot-like beak, two long horns, and spikes coming from the back of its skull. It was big too, almost 6 metres long and weighing 2 tonnes. Some of the bone fragments had been in storage since their discovery in 1958.

# TANZANIA, 2012

## GRANDADDY OF DINOSAURS FOUND IN TANZANIA

Scientists have discovered a new species of dinosaur that pre-dates any other known dinosaur by 10–15 million years! The bones, first discovered in Tanzania in the 1930s, were only recently studied in detail and were found to be 240 million years old. That puts them way back in the mid Triassic period. With only an arm bone and a few backbones to work with, not a lot is known about *Nyasasaurus parringtoni* (nye-ah-sa-saw-rus pah-ring-toh-nee). It's not clear whether this dinosaur was a carnivore or a herbivore, or even whether it walked on two legs or four, but scientists believe that this discovery provides evidence that Southern Pangaea is where dinosaurs originated.

# AUSTRALIA, 2012

### NEW AUSTRALIAN EATS MEAT!

In San Remo, Victoria, scientists have discovered bones belonging to a carnivorous theropod dinosaur of the ceratosaur family that lived 125 million years ago. The find confirms that this dinosaur group, which evolved 170 million years ago, was widespread across the supercontinent Pangaea before it broke up. Sadly, while scientists confirmed that the single ankle bone belonged to a ceratosaur, they could only guess at its appearance, but in size it may have resembled the *coelophysis* at a length of 1–3 metres, and possibly weighed in at 100 kilograms.

# MEXICO, 2012

## NEW HADROSAUR IS A HOOTER

A new hadrosaur has been discovered in Coahuila State in Northern Mexico, with the largest nasal cavities ever seen in a dinosaur. All the hadrosaurs had large noses, usually in the form of a flat snout that ended in the recognisable duckbill. However, the new discovery has huge broad cavities that suggest there may have been a pouch or bladder of some sort that could be inflated, possibly as a means of attracting or frightening away other dinosaurs. This hadrosaur has been christened *Latirhinus uitslani* (lat-tear-high-nuss ooh-eet-sla-nee), which is Greek for 'broad nose'. It most closely resembles the *Gryposaurus* (grigh-poh-saw-rus), a large duck-billed hadrosaur, and was initially mistaken for one.

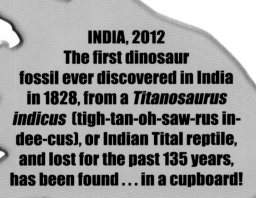

INDIA, 2012
The first dinosaur fossil ever discovered in India in 1828, from a *Titanosaurus indicus* (tigh-tan-oh-saw-rus in-dee-cus), or Indian Tital reptile, and lost for the past 135 years, has been found . . . in a cupboard!

# DINOSAUR HUNTER AWARDS

## The Dinosaur Hunter Award for the MOST ARMOURED DINOSAUR goes to ...

# Ankylosaurus!

This dinosaur from the late Cretaceous period was built like a tank. In height it wouldn't have been much taller than the average human, but it was as wide as a car, almost 6 metres in length and 6 tonnes in weight.

Ankylosaurus (an-key-loh-saw-rus) was heavily armoured all over with broad bands of spikes covering its back. A huge club at the end of its long muscular tail could be swung round hard enough to break bones on impact.

In spite of all its armour, *ankylosaurus* was a gentle herbivorous creature. The dinosaur may have spent the days grazing, safe in the knowledge that no one was going to mess with it!

# Drawing Dinosaurs

pyroraptor

Euoplocephalus

Titanosaurus

Leallynasaurus.

pyroraptor

Argentinosaurus

Spinosaurus

# GLOSSARY

## A

**allosaur**: a large bipedal carnivorous dinosaur that had a long, narrow skull and three-fingered hands; e.g. *allosaurus, australovenator, giganotosaurus*

**ankylosaur**: a heavy herbivorous quadrupedal dinosaur, normally from the Cretaceous period; e.g. *euoplocephalus, ankylosaurus, minmi*

## B

**bipedal**: capable of walking on two legs

## C

**carnivore**: meat-eater

**carnosaur**: a huge bipedal carnivorous dinosaur with small forelimbs; e.g. *allosaurus, giganotosaurus, spinosaurus*

**ceratopsian**: a frilly, horned-face herbivorous dinosaur that lived during the Cretaceous period; e.g. *albertaceratops, triceratops, pentaceratops*

**ceratosaur**: a medium-sized theropod that typically had a horned head and grasping hands with sharp claws; e.g. *coelophysis, dilophosaurus*

**coelurosaur**: a small, agile bipedal (mostly) carnivorous dinosaur, most discoveries of which have been feathered; e.g. *compsognathus, velociraptor*

**continental drift**: the gradual movement of the continents through time

**Cretaceous period**: the last period of the Mesozoic era, lasting from 145–65 million years ago

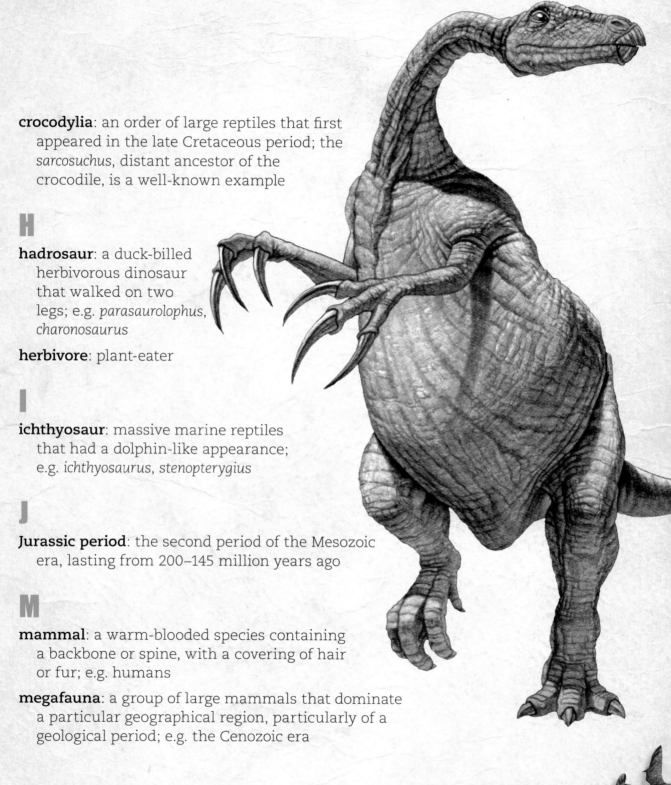

**crocodylia**: an order of large reptiles that first appeared in the late Cretaceous period; the *sarcosuchus*, distant ancestor of the crocodile, is a well-known example

## H

**hadrosaur**: a duck-billed herbivorous dinosaur that walked on two legs; e.g. *parasaurolophus*, *charonosaurus*

**herbivore**: plant-eater

## I

**ichthyosaur**: massive marine reptiles that had a dolphin-like appearance; e.g. *ichthyosaurus*, *stenopterygius*

## J

**Jurassic period**: the second period of the Mesozoic era, lasting from 200–145 million years ago

## M

**mammal**: a warm-blooded species containing a backbone or spine, with a covering of hair or fur; e.g. humans

**megafauna**: a group of large mammals that dominate a particular geographical region, particularly of a geological period; e.g. the Cenozoic era

# O

**omnivore**: eater of both plants and meat

**ornithomimosaur**: theropod dinosaurs that resembled ostriches – they were fast and were either omnivorous or herbivorous; e.g. *pelecanimimus*

**ornithopod**: a herbivorous dinosaur that had three-toed feet, which enabled them to walk erect on their hind legs; e.g. *muttaburrasaurus, iguanodon, leaellynasaura*

# P

**piscivore**: fish-eater

**plesiosaur**: a marine reptile of the Mesozoic era that had small heads, long necks, short tails and four large paddle-like flippers; e.g. *elasmosaurus*

**predator**: a creature that hunts for food (prey), normally other animals

**prey**: a creature that is hunted as food by another animal (predator)

**pterosaur**: a warm-blooded flying reptile with wings; e.g. *pterodactyl, dimorphodon, pteranodon*

## Q

**quadrupedal**: capable of walking on four legs

## S

**sauropod**: a large herbivorous quadrupedal dinosaur with a long neck and tail, small head and enormous legs; e.g. *argentinosaurus*

**supercontinent**: a great landmass that has subsequently split into smaller countries and continents; e.g. Pangaea, Gondwana and Laurasia

## T

**theropod**: a carnivorous bipedal dinosaur, whose size could range from small to large; e.g. *spinosaur, compsognathus, velociraptor*

**titanosaur**: one of the heaviest sauropod dinosaurs of the Cretaceous period; e.g. *diamantinasaurus, brachiosaurus, argentinosaurus*

**Triassic period**: the first period of the Mesozoic era, lasting from 251–200 million years ago

# INDEX

# photo credits

**Shutterstock images:** p. 6 pteranodons © Linda Bucklin; p.9 coelophylis © leonello cavetti; p.10 allosaurus ©Jean-Michel Girard; p.11 stegosaurus © Jean-Michel Girard; p.11 diplodocus © Linda Bucklin; p.12 triceratops © leonello calvetti; p.13 tyrannosaurus rex © DM7; p.14 pelicanimimus © Linda Bucklin; p.16 diamantinasaurus matildae; Linda Bucklin; p.18 euoplocephalus © Ralf Juergen Kraft; p.20 albertaceratops © Michael Rosskothen; p.22 anhanguera © Linda Bucklin; p.24 parasaurolophus © Jean-Michel Girard; p.26 argentinosaurus © Michael Rosskothen; p.20 spinosaurus © Elle Arden Images; p.30 sarcosuchus © Michael Rosskothen; p.36 museum exterior © jan kranendonk; p.37 museum interior © stocker1970; p.38 London tube train © Philip Lange; p.40 planet earth changing © plena; p.41 volcano © Sunshine Pics; p.41 broken ground © Steve Collender; p.42 Central outback © edella; p.43 mountain peak © Volodymyr Goinyk; p.43 Australia map © alehnia; p.46 museum exterior © SeanPavonePhoto; p.47 museum exterior © kai hecker p.50 mountainous landscape © photobank.kiev.ua; p.51 dimorphodon © Michael Rosskothen; p.52 pteranodon © Michael Rosskothen; p.53 archaeopteryx © Ralf Juergen Kraft; p.61 liopleurodon © Michael Rosskothen; p.62 elasmosaurus © Andreas Meyer; p.64 velociraptor © Michael Rosskothen; pp.72–73 meteor impact © sdecoret; p.74 sabre-tooth cat © Sfocato; p.75 woolly mammoth © Ozja; p.82 tuatara lizards © Cameramannz; p.82 cockroach © antpkr; p.83 alligator © Robert Eastman; p.84 dinosaur fossils © thinkdo; p.85 velociraptor © Michael Rosskothen; p.88 dinosaur fossils illustration © Andrew Chin; p.89 ankylosaurus © Catmando

**Getty images:** p.8 planocephalosaurus © DEA PICTURE LIBRARY/De Agostini Picture Library; p.9 longisquama © Jane Burton/ Warren Photographic /Photo Researchers; p.10 ichthyosaurus © Encyclopaedia Britannica/UIG/Universal Images Group; p.12 lambeosaurus © Science Photo Library/ SPL Creative; p.13 baryonyx © Gary Ombler/ Dorling Kindersley; p.32 muttaburrasaurus ©John Temperton/Dorling Kindersley RF; p.37 t-rex skeleton ©Feargus Cooney/ Lonely Planet Images; p.38 Dippy skeleton ©Latitudestock/Gallo Images; p.39 t-rex model © Chris Jackson/Getty Images Entertainment; p.45 microraptor ©Getty Images/Getty Images News; p.60 underwater floor ©Studio – Chase/Photo Researchers; p.63 archelon © DEA PICTURE LIBRARY/De Agostini Picture Library; p.70 therizinosaurus ©Joe Tucciarone/SPL/SPL Creative; p.75 megatherium ©DEA PICTURE LIBRARY/De Agostini Picture Library; p.80 tanystropheus ©De Agostini Picture Library/De Agostini; p.86 dinosaur lineup ©Science Photo Library/SPL Creative; p.87 coelyphsis © DEA PICTURE LIBRARY/De Agostini Picture Library

**Other images:** p.8 icarosaurus © Nobu Tamura (http://spinops.blogspot.com.au/) 2008; p.54 pegomastax © Todd Marshall 2011; p.74 indricotherium ©Dmitry Bogdanov 2009; p.74 glyptodon © Pavel. Riha.CB 2007

THE DISCOVERY

AMBUSH AT CISCO SWAMP

ARMOURED DEFENCE

THE DINOSAUR FEATHER

CALL OF THE WILD

DINO CHAMPIONS

DINOSAUR COVE

ERUPTION!

# Collect them all!